Take-Off!

Transport Around the World

TRUCKS

Chris Oxlade

Heinemann
LIBRARY

www.heinemann.co.uk
Visit our website to find out more information about Heinemann Library books.
To order:
 Phone 44 (0) 1865 888066
 Send a fax to 44 (0) 1865 314091
Visit the Heinemann Bookshop at www.heinemann.co.uk to browse our catalogue
and order online.

First published in Great Britain by Heinemann Library,Halley Court, Jordan Hill, Oxford C
a division of Reed Educational and Professional Publishing Ltd.
Heinemann is a registered trademark of Reed Educational and Professional Publishing Ltd.

OXFORD MELBOURNE AUCKLAND
JOHANNESBURG BLANTYRE GABORONE
IBADAN PORTSMOUTH (NH) USA CHICAGO

Designed by Paul Davies and Associates
Originated by Ambassador Litho Ltd
Printed and bound by South China Printing in Hong Kong/China

ISBN 0 431 13411 1 (hardback)   ISBN 0 431 13416 2 (paperback)
06 05 04 03 02   06 05 04 03 02
10 9 8 7 6 5 4 3 2 1   10 9 8 7 6 5 4 3 2 1

British Library Cataloguing in Publication Data

Oxlade, Chris
    Trucks. – (Transport around the world) (Take-off!)
    1.Trucks – Juvenile literature 2.Transportation, Automotive – Juvenile literature
    I.Title
    629.2'24

Acknowledgements
The publishers would like to thank the following for permission to reproduce photographs:
R D Battersby pp4, 15, 26; Trevor Clifford p10; Corbis p22; David Hoffman p23; Eye Ubiquitous pp9, 11, 13, 14, 16,
29; Pictures p27; Quadrant pp7, 12, 17, 18, 19, 24, 28; Science & Society Picture Library p8; Swift: Peter Sawell &
Partners/Freight Transport Association p6; Travel Ink: Tony Page p5; Tony Stone Images pp20, 25; John Walmsley p21

Cover photograph reproduced with permission of Alamy Images (Robert Francis).

Our thanks to Sue Graves and Hilda Reed for their advice and expertise in the preparation of this book.

Every effort has been made to contact copyright holders of any material reproduced in this book. Any omissions will
be rectified in subsequent printings if notice is given to the publishers.

Contents

Any words appearing in the text in bold, **like this**, are explained in the glossary.

What is a truck?

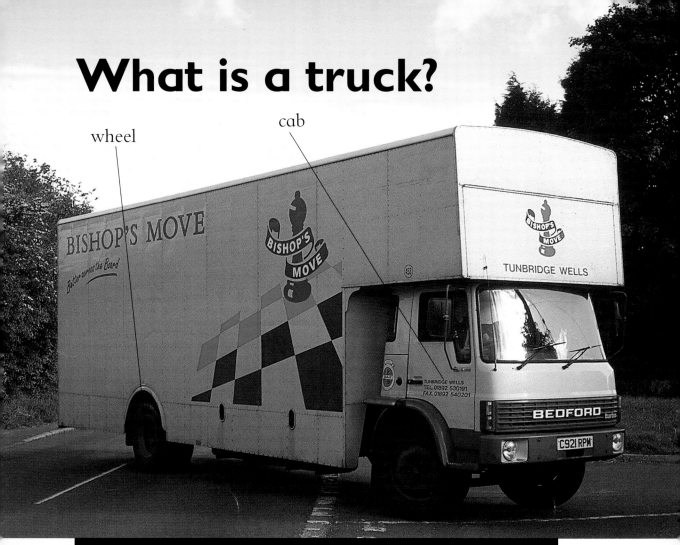

wheel

cab

BISHOP'S MOVE

Better across the Board

TUNBRIDGE WELLS

TUNBRIDGE WELLS
TEL. 01892 530191
FAX. 01892 540201

BEDFORD turbo

C921 RPW

This truck is used to move people's things to a new house.

A truck is a large **vehicle** that moves along on wheels.
Trucks carry goods called **cargo**. At the front of the
truck is a **cab** where the driver sits. At the back is a big
space for the cargo.

Trucks carry cargo to where it is needed. Then the cargo is unloaded.

Trucks were first made over 100 years ago.

cargo

truck

Cargo is being loaded onto this truck.

How trucks work

A truck has an **engine** that makes its wheels turn to move it along. It needs **fuel** to make it work.

engine

A truck's engine needs to be powerful to move heavy cargo.

rubber tyre   wheel

Trucks have air-filled rubber tyres on their wheels.

Many trucks have two wheels side by side. Some big trucks have twelve wheels or more, altogether.

A Scotsman called John Boyd Dunlop invented air-filled **rubber tyres**.

Trucks long ago

steam engine

cargo

This truck is almost 100 years old.

Before there were trucks, people used horse-drawn wagons to move **cargo**.

This **vehicle** was one of the first trucks with an engine. It is a steam engine, like the ones used in steam trains.

This small truck was made in America in the 1930s. It is called a pick-up truck. Its engine runs on **petrol**. There are many modern pick-up trucks.

Read this page again carefully. About how old is this truck?

This pick-up truck is very old.

pick-up truck

Where are trucks used?

Big trucks like this one needs a good road to travel quickly.

The smooth hard surface on roads is called tarmacadam. It was invented by John McAdam in 1815.

Big trucks carry **cargo** along main roads between towns and cities. They can travel quickly on the smooth, hard road surface.

Some trucks go through areas where there are no roads. There may be just dirt tracks and the ground can get very muddy.

The driver of this truck has decorated his cab with special designs and messages to bring him good luck on the roads!

Truck drivers know how to drive over rough ground like this.

trucks

rough ground

Flatbed trucks

ropes

Flatbed trucks have flat cargo spaces.

A truck with a flat **cargo** space is called a flatbed truck.
It can carry almost any sort of cargo. The cargo is tied in
place to stop it falling off.

crane

levers

cargo

This flatbed truck has its own small **crane** behind the **cab**. The crane lifts cargo on and off the truck. The driver works the crane by moving **levers**.

Flatbed trucks are very useful for carrying heavy building materials.

This crane can lift heavy cargo.

Articulated trucks

An articulated truck bends in the middle to make it easier to go around corners. The part where the **cargo** is carried is called a trailer.

The truck bends here.

trailer

cab

tractor unit

The front part of this truck is the tractor unit.

The part with the driver's cab and the engine is called the tractor unit. It pulls the trailer along. It can be moved from one trailer and attached to another.

Road trains

A road train is an articulated truck with two or three trailers instead of just one. There are many road trains in Australia.

Australian road trains often travel at night when it is cooler.

An Australian road train.

trailers

tractor unit

This is the inside of a road train cab.

seat   cab bed

Some cabs even have fridges and microwave ovens so that the drivers can make meals.

Road trains often travel for several days. Inside the cab there is a bed where the driver can sleep. Many trucks have curtains and cupboards too.

Tanker trucks

tank

This tanker is carrying petrol.

A tanker truck has a huge **tank** to carry **cargo**. Some tanks can be filled with liquid such as **petrol**. Other tanks carry food such as flour, grain or beans.

The tank is filled up through holes in the top. After the journey, the tank empties out through pipes at the back. The driver opens **valves** to let the cargo out.

Tankers like this deliver petrol to fuel stations.

This driver is opening valves to let petrol out.

tanker

driver

valve

Dumper trucks

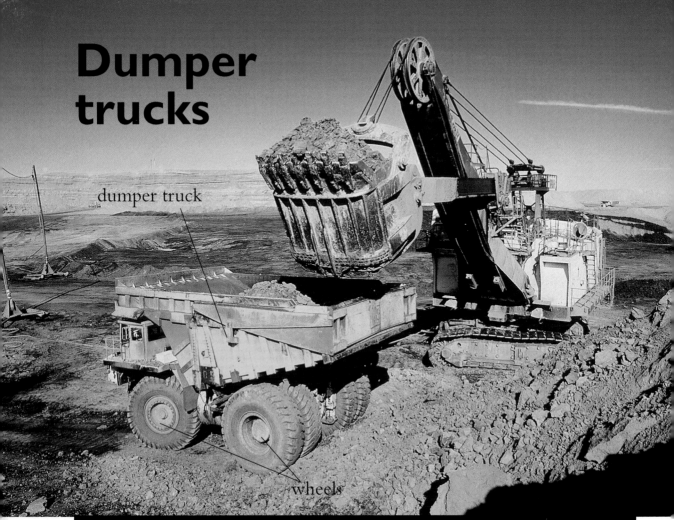

dumper truck

wheels

The huge wheels of a dumper truck can be taller than the driver!

The biggest dumper truck in the world is the Terex Titan. It can hold 550 tonnes of rubble at a time. That's the same as about 137 hippos!

Dumper trucks can be huge. Some are as tall as a house! Huge dumper trucks do not drive on roads. They work at **quarries** or building sites.

The back of a dumper truck tips up to make its **cargo** slide out on to the ground. It has powerful arms which use water pressure to push out and make the back tip. These are called hydraulic arms.

hydraulic arms

Hydraulic arms make the back of the truck tip up.

dumper truck

Rubbish trucks

This truck collects rubbish.

rubbish bin   rubbish

Many types of truck do a special job instead of carrying **cargo**. This truck goes around the streets collecting rubbish, and then takes it to a dump.

A machine lifts each rubbish bin and empties it into the back of the truck. Inside the truck, another machine crushes the rubbish to make room for more.

The machine that crushes the rubbish is called a compactor.

The machine is tipping the rubbish out of a bin into the truck.

bin

rubbish truck

machine

Snow ploughs

This snow plough is clearing ice and snow from the roads.

Old snow ploughs had studded wheels so that they would not get stuck in the snow!

During the winter, special trucks called snow ploughs keep roads open so that other **vehicles** can make their journeys safely.

At the front of the snow plough is a wide metal shovel called a plough. As the truck moves along, the plough pushes snow to the side of the road.

The plough pushes the snow to one side.

snow ploughs

plough

snow

Mobile cranes

This truck is a mobile **crane**. With its sturdy wheels and **tyres**, it can drive on roads and dirt tracks. It can move very heavy objects, such as trains onto rails.

A mobile crane is good for lifting heavy objects.

mobile crane

cab

boom

mobile crane

cab

metal feet

Metal feet stop the mobile crane from toppling over.

The boom has sections which slide into each other. This makes it easier to drive the crane from one place to another.

The crane has a long arm called a boom. It can be moved to reach high into the air. The driver works the crane from a **cab**.

Monster trucks

monster truck   old cars

People like to drive their monster trucks over obstacles.

This truck is called *Big Foot* and the one on page 29 is called *Crusher*. Why do you think they are called these names?

These **vehicles** are called monster trucks. Their owners make them from ordinary pick-up trucks. They race against each other over bumpy tracks and obstacles.

Monster trucks have huge wheels and strong **suspensions** for landing after jumps. There are strong bars inside the **cab** to protect the driver if the truck rolls over.

Monster trucks need huge wheels and strong suspensions.

wheels

suspensions

Timeline

1750 —	
	1769 Frenchman Nicholas Cugnot builds a truck to pull a huge gun. It is the first **vehicle** powered by a steam **engine**.
1800 —	
	1830s Steam-powered coaches are used in England to carry passengers between towns. But they ruin the dirt roads!
1850 —	**1850s** Steam-powered traction engines are built to pull farm machinery. Similar trucks are used to pull wagons on the roads.
	1885 The first proper car is built in Germany by Karl Benz. It has three wheels and is driven along by a petrol engine. Top speed is 13 kilometres per hour.
	1892 German engineer Rudolph Diesel develops the diesel engine. Most modern trucks have a diesel engine.
	1896 The first proper truck is built in Germany by Gottlieb Daimler. Trucks soon take over from horse-drawn wagons.
1900 —	
	1940s The first small four-wheel drive truck, called a Jeep, was built for the US army to use in World War II.
1950 —	
2000 —	

Glossary

cab   space at the front of a truck where the truck driver sits

cargo   goods that are moved from place to place

crane   machine for lifting large, heavy objects

engine   machine that uses fuel to make a vehicle move

fuel   material that is burned to make heat and power

hydraulic   moved by a liquid

lever   rod which tilts up and down or from side to side

petrol   liquid fuel used in petrol engines

quarry   place where rock is dug from the ground

rubber   soft solid material made from chemicals. It is poured into moulds to make tyres.

steam   water that has turned to a gas

suspension springs that let a truck's wheels move up and down over bumps

tank   large box-like object for storing something

tyre   rubber ring that fits around the outside of a wheel. It is filled with air.

valve   kind of tap that opens and closes to let a liquid or a gas flow or stop it flowing

vehicle   something that transports goods or people

Index